Original title:
A Juicy Life

Copyright © 2025 Creative Arts Management OÜ
All rights reserved.

Author: Aidan Marlowe
ISBN HARDBACK: 978-1-80586-293-2
ISBN PAPERBACK: 978-1-80586-765-4

Sweet Waters of Existence

In the fridge, a fruit parade,
Bananas dance in funky shades.
Celery dreams of being cool,
While carrots play the veggie fool.

Lunchboxes packed with laughter loud,
Sandwiches that look so proud.
Juice spills over, a sticky sight,
Sipping spills, we laugh in delight.

Pickles tickle the taste buds bright,
Chips make crunching sounds at night.
Ice cream bowls in a merry whirl,
Sprinkles jumping, a rainbow swirl.

So every bite brings bliss anew,
Tickling senses, tastes askew.
In this feast, we find our glee,
Living wild and free, oh me!

The Citrus Kiss of Now

Lemonade dreams dance in the sun,
The tangy giggles, oh what fun.
Orange peels in a carefree swirl,
Life's a citrus, give it a twirl.

Grapefruits chuckle as they roll,
Pineapples bounce, that's their goal.
Sweet tilts from a mango's grin,
Life's a party, let's begin!

Infusion of Joy

A blender whirls, a whacky song,
Mixing laughter, it won't be long.
Kiwi slices in a crazy line,
Happiness pours, like fresh-made wine.

Sipping sunsets at two o'clock,
Berries tumble, it's quite a shock.
Banana peels in a silly race,
Joy's a smoothie, let's embrace!

Palate of Possibilities

Tasting flavors from pie to core,
Each bite a giggle, who could ask for more?
Chocolate sprinkles on a happy day,
Life's a buffet, come join the fray.

Savory bites and sweet delight,
Cabbage laughs in the pale moonlight.
Tomato jests with a splash of zest,
Every meal's a joyful quest!

A Symphony of Flavors

Sizzling sounds and a cracking cheer,
Cooking chaos, nothing to fear.
Stirring pots like a crazy band,
Life's a concert, by taste it's planned.

Flavor notes dance on the tongue,
Mirthful munchies, forever young.
Baking breezes full of delight,
Each dish a tune, pure appetite!

The Flavor of Happiness

In a world full of sweet delight,
Bananas dance with all their might.
Pineapples spin in hula hoops,
While cherries laugh in fruity groups.

Lemons squirt with zestful cheer,
Grapefruits giggle when they're near.
Mangoes wear their brightest smiles,
And oranges gossip for a while.

Orchard of Opportunities

In a garden ripe with silly dreams,
Peaches sing in sunshine beams.
Plums are bouncing, full of glee,
As apples plan a jamboree.

Strawberries throw a juicy bash,
While raspberries giggle and splash.
Every fruit has fun to spare,
Creating joy beyond compare.

Lush Revelations

Coconuts crack with tales untold,
While figs reveal their secrets bold.
Pomegranates share their seeds of fate,
And avocados won't be late.

Grapes are rolling, making bets,
On which will win the juiciest sets.
Fruit salad dreams are what they crave,
In this orchard, they're all brave.

Bursting with Potential

With every bite, a giggle grows,
As melons burst with sweet prose.
Kiwi whispers with a wink,
While bananas ride their pink ink.

Tangerines tumble down the lane,
Squeezing laughter, skipping mundane.
Every snack is pure delight,
Fruity foes in a playful fight.

Overflowing with Essence

Life's a fruit stand, what a sight,
Banana peels in broad daylight.
Pick a melon, pass the lime,
Every bite's a punchline, every time.

Juicy oranges, giggling bright,
Chasing squirrels, what a delight.
Pineapples wear fancy hats,
Sugar-coated laughter, where's the cat?

Palate of Experiences

Taste the rainbow on your plate,
Cupcakes dance, they can't wait.
Caramel rivers, oh what fun,
Belly laughs, we weigh a ton!

Pickle-flavored jellybeans,
Silly dreams and wobbly scenes.
Munching dreams like popcorn kernels,
Tickled toes and jam-filled journals.

Juxtaposed Flavors of Life

Sweet and sour, tasting fate,
Lemon drops, oh how they rate!
Chili chocolate, spicy twist,
In this kitchen, who could resist?

Marshmallow clouds, gummy bears,
Sailing boats in lemonade chairs.
Mix it up, shake and stir,
Every flavor wants a whir!

Harvesting Moments of Wonder

Pick your apple, spin around,
Giggles echo, laughter's found.
Cotton candy clouds float high,
Grab a slice of pumpkin pie!

Berries burst, a juicy bomb,
Chasing fireflies, oh what calm.
Moments ripe, like grapes in sun,
Life's a feast, let's have some fun!

The Sweetness of Each Day

Wake up each morning, looking for a treat,
Cereal with sprinkles, a breakfast so sweet.
Socks mismatched dancing, my style's a delight,
Spilling my coffee, but that's all right!

Chasing the mailman, just for a wave,
I trip on my shoelace, how silly and brave.
Neighbors all chuckle, they know me too well,
Life's just a circus, with stories to tell.

Harvesting Moments

In the garden of laughter, I plant some fun,
With fruit made of giggles, we're never done.
Carrots in costumes, dancing with glee,
Tomatoes are blushing, oh can't you see?

We gather our whispers, like apples in autumn,
Each joke is a treasure, and oh, how we've fought 'em!
With each silly blooper, our hearts grow more wide,
Picking joy from the branches, it's quite the ride!

Fruitful Dreams

Dreams like ripe berries, bursting with cheer,
Whimsical wishes, we hold them all near.
Banana peels slipping, oh dear, what a sight,
We tumble and giggle, what pure delight!

The clouds sprinkle laughter like sugar on cakes,
Riding on rainbows, dodging the brakes.
With each silly hiccup, we chase after glee,
Gathering memories, wild and free!

Zest of the Now

Squeeze every second like lemonade fresh,
With friends making faces, a joyful mess!
Chasing our shadows, out under the sun,
Life's a bold flavor, let's all have some fun!

In the whirl of our laughter, time starts to spin,
Grinning at mishaps, we always win.
So grab a moment and shake it around,
In this zesty adventure, pure joy can be found!

Flavors of the Forgotten

There's a taste of gloom in the fridge,
Pickles have turned, now they're a smidge.
A smoothie of socks, a sauce of regret,
Dining on these? I'm not placing my bet.

Old bread on the shelf mocks my plight,
It's bread, it's alive, it's planning a flight.
The ketchup upright, a lonesome king,
Crying out for fries, or a savory fling.

The Zest of Living Boldly

Lemons squeeze dreams in a bold parade,
Dancing with limes, a citrus charade.
But watch your step, on the zest you glide,
One slip, and you're a pie in the tide.

Bananas in pajamas on a wild spree,
Slip on their peels? Oh, woe is me!
Mangoes wearing hats, quite the debonair,
Inviting all fruits for a daring affair.

A Feast of Vibrant Dreams

Green beans in tuxedos, cherry on top,
Carrots tap dancing, they just won't stop.
Fridge full of laughter, it's all quite ripe,
Spaghetti in bow ties adds to the hype.

Chocolate rivers flow beneath the moon,
Candy canes waltz, a dandy cartoon.
Berries in sundresses twirl on the stage,
A feast for the senses, like turning a page.

Ripe with Possibilities

A peach has a secret beneath its bold skin,
Whispers of sweetness, where do I begin?
Tangerine dreams roll down the street,
Offering slices of their sun-kissed beat.

Pineapple wears shades, feeling divine,
Sipping on coconut, straight from the brine.
In this fruity tale, laughs grow on trees,
Biting into giggles, we dance in the breeze.

Euphoria in Every Drop

Sipping soda, fizz so bright,
My dentist cringes with each bite.
Chasing ice cream down the street,
Happiness scooped, oh what a treat!

Lemonade spills down my chin,
Life's too short, let's just dive in.
Pies in windows, such a sight,
Crusty dreams take off in flight!

Nectar of the Everyday

Coffee stains on sleepy mug,
Morning hugs, oh how they tug!
Syrup drips from pancakes tall,
Sticky fingers, love it all!

Cherries dance on frosty bowls,
Silly giggles fill our souls.
Whipped cream fights with juicy fruit,
Messy joy, oh what a hoot!

Savored Moments on the Palate

Chocolate cakes that tempt and tease,
Crumbling crumbs that beg and please.
Popcorn showers at the show,
Salty kernels steal the show!

Donuts sprout from every shop,
Sugar rush, I'll never stop!
In every bite, a story told,
Life's flavors vibrant, bright and bold!

Bursting with Flavor

Pickles crunch like laughter loud,
Sandwich stacks that make me proud.
Fruit kabobs that laugh and play,
Juicy bites lead us astray!

Tacos piled with all the zest,
Salsa ladders, who's the best?
Lemon drops that spin around,
Life's a party, joy is found!

Cascade of Flavors

In the kitchen, pots are dancing,
Beetroot throwing a wild prancing.
Carrots giggle, peas all grin,
Sauce splatters like a playful sin.

Herbs are whispering secret tunes,
Basil twirls beneath the moons.
Garlic sneezes, oh what a show,
While onions take their turn to glow.

A splash of lemon, a pinch of zest,
Every bite feels like a fest.
Taste buds tumble, hearts will sing,
Who knew veggies could party this spring!

Dinner plates all stacked so high,
Wait, don't eat—just let them lie,
This feast of colors, soft and bright,
Turns every meal into pure delight.

The Sweet Shade of Joy

Underneath a big green tree,
Lemons laugh, come join with me.
Strawberries play tag and hide,
Ripe bananas lean with pride.

Melons bounce like old-time balls,
Grapes giggle as each one falls.
Coconut jokes, a hairy tease,
Tickling taste buds like a breeze.

Juice drips down with every bite,
Sweetness soaring, pure delight.
Fruits having fun, what a sight,
Nature's candy takes to flight.

Lemonade dreams in sunshine cheer,
Sips of joy, we hold so dear.
Chilling drinks with friends so near,
The sweet shade of laughs and beer.

Bursting Bounties

Berries bouncing in the bowl,
Each one claiming its own role.
Raspberries yell, 'Pick me now!'
While blueberries take a bow.

Cherry jokes with a little tang,
Limes yell out, 'I'm in the gang!'
Fruits unite, a funny bunch,
They burst with laughter at lunchtime crunch.

Jams on toast, a sticky cheer,
Spreading joy from ear to ear.
Waffles dance with syrup swirls,
As pancake towers start to twirl.

In this feast, there's no defeat,
Every morsel feels so sweet.
From summer's garden, life's a brawl,
Bursting bounties, we share it all.

Flavors of Freedom

Out in the world, flavors fly,
Savory spices reach for the sky.
Pickles giggle, chips all cheer,
Bringing freedom, far and near.

BBQ sauce with a bold remark,
Sizzling burgers make their mark.
Tacos dancing in sheer delight,
Each one brimming, what a sight!

Sauce on sleeves, a messy grin,
Fried treats making us dive in.
Spinach rolls in a funky dress,
They declare, 'We eat to impress!'

Chili peppers hold a fight,
Making taste buds dance all night.
With laughter echoing, let's all say,
Flavors of freedom light the way!

Citrus Dreams

In a grove filled with sun,
Lemons laugh, having fun.
Oranges tango, dance in cheer,
Grapefruits join, sipping beer.

Pineapples wear sunglasses bright,
Limes throw parties, day and night.
All together, they make a scene,
Juicy joy, a citrus dream.

The Taste of Tomorrow

Kiwis chat about their flair,
Bananas swing without a care.
Strawberries gossip, red and sweet,
Mangoes boast, they can't be beat.

Papayas plot a party soon,
Peaches hum a silly tune.
In the fridge, it's a wild race,
Taste bud party, oh what a place!

Vibrancy in Every Bite

Watermelon winks, all so bright,
Cherries giggle, what a sight!
Grapes roll around, causing a mess,
With every bite, there's pure happiness.

Pears share secrets, juicy delight,
Avocados bring guacamole light.
Life's a feast, let flavors unite,
In every bite, pure sheer delight.

Juicy Echoes

Berries bounce on a fruity spree,
Dancing around, wild and free.
Each one shouts, 'Take a risk!'
In a world of flavor, it's a brisk.

Pineapples joke, 'We're the best!'
Mangoes boast, 'Forget the rest!'
Echoes of laughter, sweetness so bright,
In this fruit kingdom, all feels right.

The Melodies of Life

In a world where laughter sings,
Bouncing berries burst with zing.
Banana peels on the floor wait,
Making every step a twist of fate.

Dancing pies with whipped cream hats,
Chasing squirrels, oh, what of that!
Grapes giggle as they roll away,
Hiding in the sun, oh, what a play!

Sippin' nectar from a straw,
Dripping sweetness, oh, what a flaw!
Strawberries wearing tiny hats,
Riding to the fridge with the chitchats.

Berry baskets cheer with glee,
As fruit flies get their degree.
Life's a wink, a twist, a spin,
Where the fun begins, let's win!

Serenade of Sweetness

Syrup rivers flow and gleam,
In a waffle world, we dream.
Cheesy puns on every plate,
Making mealtimes never late.

Frothy coffees, a frolicsome wave,
Muffins dance, mischief they crave.
The frosting plays hide and seek,
While the cookies giggle and squeak.

Nutty bars in a wacky race,
Trying to win the snacktime space.
Pancakes flop with syrupy lands,
While we munch with sticky hands.

Sweet pies promise happy cheers,
With every bite, melt away fears.
Life's a treat, a tasty jest,
Join the fun—who's eating best?

Fragrant Journeys

Lemon zest on the travel route,
Bringing joy, oh, what a hoot!
Whiff of cookies in the breeze,
Pies take flight with utmost ease.

Cherry blossoms flap their wings,
While chocolate bunnies strut and sing.
Through fields of magenta and green,
Life's essence is sticky and keen.

Cinnamon rolls in cozy homes,
Making music as it roams.
Hoagies bounce from bread's embrace,
No blandness in this wild chase!

Sausage links race in a line,
With giggles as they do their time.
Embrace the scents that swirl and swoon,
In this banquet of a cartoon!

Colorful Bites of Existence

Kaleidoscope of fruit on display,
Every bite's a bright ballet.
Sneaky veggies wear disguise,
Hiding in the snack surprise.

Gummy bears plotting with glee,
Jumping through a candy spree.
Cotton candy clouds all around,
In this sugary world, joy is found.

Pickles in shades of zesty green,
Tapping toes like a festive scene.
Cheeseburgers don a spice parade,
With flavors so bold, how can we fade?

Rainbow sprinkles swaying in time,
Creating laughter, oh so sublime.
Life's a buffet full of delights,
With colors and crunch that excite our nights!

Savoring Sorrows

When life hands you lemons on a spree,
Just squirt them on fish and sip your tea.
The tears we shed are just dressing, you see,
So laugh with the clouds, let your worries flee.

In pickle-brined mornings, I ponder and stare,
With doughnuts! Oh, life's such a whimsical dare.
So sprinkle your days with sweet laughter and flair,
And dance with your shadows, in bright underwear.

The Richness of Dreams

In the land of sleep, there are chocolate streams,
With rivers of candy and marshmallow beams.
Every whimsy whispers, or so it seems,
That life's just a pie, bursting at the seams.

Glimpses of fortune, with muffins in hand,
Sprinkling joy like a fruity bandstand.
The riches of dreams are all perfectly planned,
And laughter erupts like a pop in the sand.

Zesty Encounters

Meeting a lime on my stroll yesterday,
It shouted, "Be fabulous!" in a citrusy way.
With salsa and salsa, we danced in dismay,
A spicy old tango, come join the buffet!

Bumping into garlic, it said with a wink,
"Life's zest is more potent when you don't overthink!"
With flavors and fun, there's no room to stink,
Let's guzzle the joy, with a wink and a drink!

The Flavor of Hope

The cherry on top of a sundae so bright,
Is hope, like sprinkles, that sparkles at night.
Bite into tomorrow, sweet morsels of light,
And discover that flavors can bring pure delight.

Ice cream dreams swirl in the warmth of the sun,
With laughter that bubbles, like soda, just fun.
So scoop up your troubles, and don't you outrun,
The flavor of hope, when life's just begun!

Succulent Tales of Joy

In the land of lollipops, life's a treat,
Where cupcakes dance on sugar-sweet feet.
Rainbows sprinkle every sunny day,
And laughter bubbles in a silly display.

With jello pools and licorice trees,
Pineapple moonbeams float on the breeze.
Syrup rivers twist and twirl,
In this whimsical, wobbly world.

Silly socks on wacky feet prance,
While gummy bears invite you to dance.
With sprinkles flying high like confetti,
Joy's a game that's always ready.

So grab a friend, and take the ride,
On life's goofy, giggly side.
Let the good times overflow,
In this land where smiles always glow.

The Essence of Colorful Living

Life's a canvas, splashed with hues,
Where oranges sing and grape wine stews.
With candy clouds and soda pop streams,
Chasing joy is more than it seems.

Lemons giggle and cucumbers grin,
Dancing on tables, inviting us in.
With each bite of cake, a new delight,
Life's a festival, a sweet bite!

Mangoes play tag with the cantaloupe crew,
Watermelon secrets, oh what a view!
Fruits in hats brewed up with cheer,
Every moment, a juicy frontier.

So let's paint the world with our quirkiest ways,
With spritzer laughter to brighten our days.
Life's a feast, so gather around,
In this banquet of joy, happiness abounds.

Juicy Connections

Friends like cherries, sweeter when shared,
Slicing life, we're joyfully paired.
Banana peels and silly slips,
With every giggle, our friendship flips.

Berries tumble in a friendly game,
Each burst of laughter has no shame.
Fruit salads made of silly tales,
Connecting hearts like fun-filled trails.

Together we squeeze the zest from our days,
With a splash of humor in playful ways.
Like fizzy drinks that tickle and sing,
Our juicy bond is an endless spring.

So raise a toast with your favorite squeeze,
To connections that flow just like the breeze.
In this orchard of love, let's take a dive,
With every laugh, we feel so alive!

Richness in Every Breath

Inhale the laughter, exhale the fun,
Life's a carnival, a cheeky run.
Bubbles pop in the air above,
Each breath a treasure, a gift of love.

Sip the sweetness, taste the sun's rays,
Dance to the rhythm of joyous plays.
With every giggle, we plump up our souls,
In this buffet of life, we strive for our goals.

Grapefruit mornings, zesty and bright,
Sparkling evenings, filled with delight.
With each heartbeat, we toast to the thrill,
Life's juicy essence, the ultimate fill.

So let's breathe in the wonders that glow,
Each moment a richness, let laughter flow.
In this tapestry woven with cheer,
Every breath's a party, let's shift into gear!

Rich Flavors of Being

Life's a buffet, tastes galore,
Eat your cake, then ask for more!
Sprinkle joy on every dish,
Don't forget dessert—make a wish!

Baked beans and silly songs,
Dancing all where we belong.
Mixing flavors, laugh out loud,
Join the quirkiest of crowd!

Grab a pickle, dip and swirl,
Every bite's a little twirl.
Salsa moves with every taste,
Never let a chance go waste!

In this feast, your groove will show,
Life's a punchline, let it flow.
Share your plate, don't let it wane,
Savor puns like sweet champagne!

Savoring Simplicity

In a world of glitz and glam,
I find joy in peanut butter jam.
Ketchup smiles, mustard grins,
Who knew lunch could lead to wins?

Peas in pods and corny jokes,
Simple joys like happy folks.
Lemonade spills under the sun,
Sipping sweetness, just for fun!

Gather the crumbs, don't fuss, my friend,
Simplicity is on the mend!
A sandwich made with love and cheer,
Tastes much better with friends near.

Chocolate syrup on my nose,
Life's great, when you never pose!
Grab a spoon, just make a mess,
In this chaos, you'll feel blessed!

Tasting the Colors of Life

Life's a canvas, paint it bright,
Strawberry dreams take flight at night.
Zesty lime with giggles swirl,
Sip the rainbow, give it a whirl!

Jellybeans and bubblegum,
Taste the colors, here they come!
Blue raspberry, lemon yellows,
Every flavor makes us fellows!

Skittles sky, a tart parade,
Gummy bears are never afraid.
Candy sunsets with comical flair,
Life's a fairground, laughter in air!

Orange giggles, grape surprise,
Every munch under laughter skies.
Plum-tastic days, let's play and stay,
In this carnival, munch away!

Vibrant Harvest

The orchard's ripe, let's dance around,
Pickin' apples with goofy sounds.
Pumpkin hats and carrot ties,
Harvest moon and silly pies!

Baskets full of whimsy fruits,
Skip around in fluffy boots.
Cherries wink, grapes start to roll,
Life's a harvest, bless your soul!

Corny jokes in every patch,
Sunflower crowns, let's make a match.
Squash the worries, don't be glum,
Swing together, sing a hum!

In the fields of purple hue,
Let's embrace the funny crew.
Life's a feast of golden dreams,
With every joke, it merrily beams!

Whimsical Harvests

In a garden of giggles, tomatoes grow,
They dance in the breeze, putting on a show.
Carrots wear shades, and onions do cheer,
With every pluck, there's laughter, oh dear!

Cabbages gossip about the peas,
While radishes nudge and tickle the bees.
Lettuce gets soggy from too much delight,
As sunflowers bask in the warm, golden light.

Pumpkins wear hats that are comically huge,
Scarecrows tell tales to the bewildered gnoos.
Fruits groove on branches, feeling quite spry,
Who knew vegetables could reach for the sky?

Baskets overflows with humor and cheer,
As the harvest brings joy, we all draw near.
So let's plant a joke and water it right,
And laugh till we burst, oh what a sight!

The Palette of Life

Life's a canvas splashed with bright fruit hues,
Painting our days with laughter and snooze.
Strawberries giggle while grapes roll away,
Each color tells stories of fun in the fray.

Bananas wear smiles, oh what a sight,
While peaches and nectarines hold laughter tight.
In this colorful kitchen, we'll stir up delight,
A saucy concoction to brighten the night.

Carrots in aprons, they chop and they slice,
As berries bounce in, oh, isn't that nice?
The salad gets silly with herbs having fun,
Dancing around till the day is done.

So mix up your joy, let the flavors collide,
With each tart giggle, your worries can hide.
In this joyous banquet, let's all raise a toast,
To the palette of laughter, we cherish the most!

Sweet Surprises

Under the surface of apples so red,
Lie secrets and giggles that tickle your head.
Bite into sweetness, the crunch sings a tune,
While cherries conspire to dance 'neath the moon.

Peaches in pajamas, oh what a sight,
Whispering softly to grapes, holding tight.
Lemon drops roll and giggle in packs,
Sour to sweet, they'll launch playful attacks.

In a picnic basket, delight takes the lead,
S'mores stack high like a prideful steed.
Surprises abound with each crunchy bite,
Who knew snack time could spark such delight?

So gather your friends and spread out the cloth,
With fruit-flavored laughter, let worries go froth.
In this garden of goodness, we savor each jest,
For sweetness is fleeting, let's eat with zest!

Melon-Soft Whispers

Melons whisper secrets in the summer's warm shade,
With hushed giggles floating, their doubts are outweighed.
Watermelon winks with a juicy delight,
While cantaloupes chuckle, all through the night.

Honeydews lounge, wearing sun hats so bright,
Their laughter is sweet, such a refreshing sight.
The picnic is buzzing with fruity romance,
As mangoes and kiwis break into a dance.

Slicers on hand, we gather around,
Each piece tells a story as laughter abounds.
With sticky fingers and smiles that won't fade,
Melon-soft whispers make memories invade.

So let's feast on this joy, with bowls piled high,
To the sweet, silly wonders that flutter and fly.
In this fruit-filled frolic, together we shine,
For life's all about sweetness and laughter divine!

Abundant Waters

A splash of color, oh what a mess,
My drink now tastes like a fruit dress.
Lemons and limes dance in the glass,
Sipping so hard, I hope I don't pass!

Waterfalls of giggles spill over my cup,
Fruits float around, like they're drowning up!
Vodka or tonic, I can't really tell,
Either way, cheers to life; here's wishing you well.

From smoothies to punches, oh what a ride,
With every new fruity friend by my side.
Mixing and stirring, we're shaking it right,
Raise your glass high and twirl in delight!

Catch a swim in the flavor, dive deep,
Forget all the worries, just laugh - don't weep!
Life's a big pitcher, pour it out loud,
In this watery bliss, we're all a bit proud!

Exuberant Essence

Pumpkin spice lattes in sunshine's gleam,
Waffles with syrup, oh what a dream!
Can't stop the giggles from tickling my soul,
Doughnuts and sprinkles, let's roll, let's roll!

Tacos that whisper, "Come take a bite,"
Crispy and crunchy, they're pure delight.
Salsa on table, it's wiggle and sway,
Chips uplifting me, hip hip hooray!

Chocolatey goodness, it's calling my name,
Each happy mouthful, a sweet kind of game.
Dashing through flavors, like I'm in bliss,
What's life without sugar? God bless this kiss!

Cakes that are layered, like stories untold,
Mouthfuls of joy, they never grow old.
With every bite shared, let smiles ignite,
Living the essence; oh what a sight!

The Tang of Time

There once was a lime who lived in my fridge,
Looking a bit sour, just like a bridge.
I thought, "What to do with this zesty old crate?"
Then mixed him with gin - oh, now that's fate!

Time flew on by like a fruit fly's dance,
Squeezed out the sweet, gave my drink a chance.
Pineapples laughing, and cherries so bright,
Drinking this time, it feels just right!

Sandwiches stacked like a Jenga tower,
Tomatoes and lettuce, overflowing power.
Ketchup that giggles, mustard that sings,
It's brunch time, baby! Oh, what joy it brings!

Spices in whirlwinds, a taste that's sublime,
Let's spice up the minutes with every lime!
In this tangy magic, let's savor each chime,
Forever and ever, the zest of our time!

Cravings for Connection

I crave a hot dog, that's finished with flair,
Ketchup, and mustard, they float in the air.
Fried onions tumble, like tumbleweed,
Together we feast; our hearts are freed!

Pizza parties spark joy, like fireworks bright,
Cheese, oh so stretchy, it's love at first bite.
Sharing a slice or two, laughing and cheer,
Friends in the kitchen, the party is here!

Ice cream is dancing, with sprinkles on top,
Melting and swirling, I just can't stop.
Sundaes that giggle with laughter and glee,
Let's dig in deep, like a fruit-filled spree!

The snack table beckons, "Come join in the fun!"
Chips and guacamole, we've only begun.
Together our cravings, a feast for the soul,
In every connection, we bloom and we roll!

The Aroma of Dreams

In a land where flavors dance,
We chase the scents, a merry prance.
With donuts on trees and pies in the sky,
We laugh and eat, oh my, oh my!

Giant lollipops on the candy road,
Each step a giggle, a sugary load.
We sip from fountains, soda so sweet,
Life's a banquet, come take a seat!

Rainbows sprout in fizzy streams,
Chocolate rivers, oh what dreams!
With each gulp, our worries fade,
In this blissful, edible parade!

So join the feast, don't be shy,
With forks of joy, we'll reach the sky.
And in this land of tasty schemes,
We'll twirl and whirl inside our dreams!

Quenching Thirst for Wonder

Oh what a thirst, for laughs and cheer,
A soda spritz, we hold so dear.
With every sip, a giggle flows,
As bubbles tickle, joy bestows!

In a carnival of flavor, we race,
A wild goose chase, ogling each face.
With skewers of fruit, we toast our luck,
While pies fly by, it's a fruitcake truck!

A zesty lemon whispers a joke,
While pickle pops tease and provoke.
With every chomp, a song we hum,
These juicy moments make our hearts drum!

Raise your cup in a fizzy cheer,
Let's quench our thirst, we've no fear.
In this world, where wonder spins,
We laugh and feast as life begins!

Slices of Bliss

Life serves slices, oh what a treat,
With cheese that squeaks, it can't be beat.
We gobble up giggles, lick our plates,
In this buffet, of oddball fates!

Pineapple hats and grape-like shoes,
Dancing with veggies, oh what a snooze!
With whipped cream clouds in a donuts sky,
We snack and nap, oh my oh my!

Jellybean rains, a sweet surprise,
While chocolate bunnies wear silly ties.
Every bite's a roll of the dice,
Living in a whimsy paradise!

So grab your fork, don't you fret,
A slice of joy, our best bet yet.
We feast on giggles, we savor bliss,
In our scrumptious, silly abyss!

Ripe Realities

In gardens of laughter, ripe fruits sway,
Life's a cocktail, mix and play.
With splashes of fun, in every task,
We pluck the moments, no need to ask!

Banana peels and jelly jars,
With starry nights and candy cars.
We ride the waves, of fizzy bliss,
Chasing after the world's sweetest kiss!

Yes, life is fruity, incredibly grand,
With giggles and grins, hand in hand.
So give it a squeeze, don't let it slip,
Taste every moment, take a big dip!

In this juicy chaos, we raise a cheer,
For ripe realities that bring us near.
We dance with joy, we leap and shout,
In this splendid feast, there's never doubt!

Juiced Aspirations

I dream of rivers made of fruit,
Where lemons dance and limes salute.
Strawberries in slippers, they waltz all night,
While carrots play cards, what a sight!

The apples throw a party, so grand,
With juicy punch served by banana band.
Kiwis juggling limes in the air,
While pineapples laugh without a care!

Cucumbers in tuxedos spin round,
In this zesty kingdom, joy is found.
With each sip of fun, I take a chance,
The fruit parade leads me to dance!

So here's to life, all squeezed and chewed,
The zest within, can't be subdued.
In my blender dreams, I shall reside,
In the whirlwind joy, I take my ride.

Garden of Joy

In a garden plot where giggles grow,
I plant my seeds of laughter, you know.
Tomatoes wear hats, dressed to impress,
While beans do the cha-cha, no less!

With carrots as chums, they tickle the ground,
Radishes rhyme, oh what a sound!
Peas in their pods, they just can't wait,
For the dance-off that's center-stage fate.

Butterflies buzzing, sipping on dew,
Painting the petals in colors so true.
In this merry patch where smiles meet,
Grows the recipe for joy, oh so sweet!

So come take a stroll, smell the blooms,
Among this bliss, passion resumes.
We'll harvest laughter as we chase,
In this jovial place, we'll embrace!

Sourcing Sunshine

From the kitchen window, the sun peeks in,
He whispers softly, 'Let the fun begin!'
Toast pirouetting in buttery glee,
While coffee winks at my sleepy spree.

Freshly squeezed orange laughs from the bowl,
Tickling my taste buds, igniting my soul.
A splash of strawberry with sprightly flair,
Setting my spirits free in the air!

There's a pancake stack that's ready to dive,
Into syrup rivers where sweet dreams thrive.
With giggles and grins, oh what a sight,
Let's feast on sunshine 'til the night!

So let the morning keep brewing delight,
With every bite, let laughter take flight.
Together we'll savor all this zest,
In the warmth of joy, we are truly blessed!

The Splash of Liveliness

Jumping in puddles of fruity delight,
Where lemons swing by with all of their might.
Berries take turns in a whirlpool spree,
Creating waves of laughter, just let it be!

Mangoes in spandex performing a show,
While grapes cheer them on in a row.
Every splash tells a story, you see,
Of a fruit medley wild and carefree!

Splashing and splashing, let's dive right in,
With watermelon smiles, we all begin.
A conga of colors, so full of glee,
In this ocean of flavor, come splash with me!

So let's raise our glasses of fizzy fun,
For life's just a party under the sun.
With every zing and zesty embrace,
We'll ride the waves of this playful space.

Radiant Reflections

In the mirror, I dance with glee,
My hair's a mess, but that's just me.
I wear my fruit hat with pride,
Strawberries waving like I'm bonafide.

A squirt of lime, a dash of fun,
Sips of chaos when I run.
Bananas slipping here and there,
My life's a show, I'm unaware!

Lemons giggle in the sun,
Jokes are ripe, oh what a pun!
I juggle oranges, what's the score?
Each day's a laugh, who could want more?

As I stroll through laughter's lane,
I chase the spritz, I love the rain.
With a blender whirling, hear it sing,
My vibrant life is the real zing!

The Drink of Dreams

There's a cup that holds my wishes,
Full of laughter, served with dishes.
Sparkling soda, a splash of cheer,
It's party time, when friends are near!

Come take a sip of my delight,
With fizzy bubbles, we take flight.
Peaches dancing in the foam,
Every gulp feels like home!

A twist, a shake, let's not forget,
Garish umbrellas — my best bet.
Lemonade wishes and minty dreams,
Life taste-tests, or so it seems.

My drink of dreams is never plain,
With gummy bears that dance in rain.
So grab a glass and skip the grind,
A swirling funhouse waits to find!

Life's Bold Infusions

In a whirl of hopes, I dive right in,
Chili peppers give my heart a spin.
Tangled noodles, I devour fast,
Each tasty bite, a joyous blast!

Colorful spices, a pinch of flair,
Mixing flavors, with quirky care.
Garlic whispers secrets sweet,
Every dish a treat to eat!

Croutons leap from bowls to skies,
Every crunch brings comical sighs.
I toast my bread with roasted seeds,
Life's fusion feeds my fun-filled needs!

Broths that bubble, laughter's stew,
Simmering dreams, a hearty brew.
Culinary magic, what a thrill,
Life's bold infusions, splendid fill!

Sips of Happiness

A slushy sight, oh what a drink,
Berries swirling, pink and wink.
Each sip's a giggle, smiles galore,
With rainbow straws, who could want more?

Sugar's sweet and laughter's loud,
I toast alone, but feel so proud.
Cherries popping in the glow,
Every gulp, a happy show!

Sipping joy in a fancy cup,
Whipped cream mountains, can't get enough!
Sprinkles tumble like laughter free,
In this joyride, come sip with me!

With every swallow, the world's a cheer,
Blending flavors that we hold dear.
Raise your glass to the neon light,
Sips of happiness, oh what a sight!

Cravings of the Heart

When chocolate calls, I can't resist,
A sweetened hug that I can't miss.
Cakes and pies, they dance around,
In sugar-coated dreams, I'm tightly bound.

Oh, pizza slices, so cheesy and warm,
With toppings galore, they break the norm.
My heart does flutter with every bite,
In the battle of cravings, I'll always fight.

Ice cream rivers, flowing so proud,
In waffle boats, I cheer out loud.
Each scoop a smile, my taste buds sing,
In this carnival of food, I'm the king.

So here's to munching, crunching with glee,
With every nibble, I'm wild and free.
My heart's a buffet, a humorous spree,
Who knew that joy could taste so zany?

The Orchard of Existence

In a orchard of laughter, fruits hang low,
Bananas chuckle, apples steal the show.
Pears gossip softly, in leafy disguise,
While oranges wink with citrusy lies.

Grapes giggle as they tumble around,
While berries burst forth in colorful sound.
Every bite brings a comical cheer,
In this fruity world, happiness is near.

With watermelon whispers and berry bling,
Every harvest day feels like a fling.
My basket's a treasure of juicy delight,
In this orchard, each moment feels light.

So come take a stroll, let laughter prevail,
In the land of the silly, we'll laugh without fail.
Each fruit tells a tale, so wild and grand,
In the orchard of life, let's all make a stand!

Sips of Sunshine

Lemonade rivers, with rays that glint,
On thirsty days, it's the perfect hint.
With bubbles of laughter in every glass,
A sip of sunshine, let worries pass.

Mango magic in smoothies swirl,
Each straw a journey, each sip a twirl.
Pineapple boast, in its tropical flair,
With refreshing giggles that fill the air.

Coconut whispers, in chilled delight,
Like beachy vacations, everything's right.
A splash of spritz, a hint of zest,
In my cup of cheer, I'm surely blessed.

So raise your drinks, let's toast this spree,
In each little drop, find the joy that's free.
Life is a party, let's sip it slow,
With sips of sunshine, let laughter flow!

Nectar of Existence

Buzzing around, the bees hum a tune,
As flowers giggle beneath the moon.
Honey drips down like warm, sweet gold,
In life's little moments, treasures unfold.

A spoonful of joy, stirred in my tea,
With every sip, I feel so free.
Jar of sweet memories, sticky and bright,
Life's nectar glistens in morning light.

While syrupy tales weave thick and sweet,
With pancakes piling, oh what a feat!
In the breakfast dance, we laugh and twirl,
With nectar and laughter, give life a whirl.

So gather your bees, let the sweetness soar,
Let's cherish these moments, and always want more.
For in this wild world, so bizarre yet true,
The nectar of life is made for me and you!

The Sweetness of Now

Grab your shades, let's hit the sun,
The time is ripe for silly fun.
Watermelons giggle, apples grin,
Dancing with joy, let the feast begin!

Juice drips down, a sticky mess,
But laughter reigns, we feel so blessed.
Caught in fruit fights, we squeal with glee,
Who knew dessert could set us free?

Pineapples wear crowns, oh so proud,
Telling jokes, drawing a crowd.
Bananas slip, but we don't care,
Life's best moments happen everywhere!

So let's toast with our sparkling drink,
To juicy laughs, don't you think?
Let the good times roll, get off the ground,
In this tasty now, joy can be found!

Savoring Sunlit Days

Picnic blankets under bright blue skies,
Sandwiches dancing, oh what a surprise!
Lemonade rivers flow with a cheer,
While ants march in, oh dear, oh dear!

Sunblock battles, who's the white ghost?
Straws that twirl like a silly host.
Hot dogs smile, take a big bite,
While ketchup and mustard start a fight!

Ice cream cones stand tall and proud,
Scoops that melt in a giggling crowd.
Dripping sweetness runs down our hands,
Life's little joys, our favorite brands!

So let's play games till the sun bows low,
Dance in the twilight, let the laughter flow.
We'll wrap up the day in a fruity haze,
Savoring life in these sunlit days!

Lush Adventures Await

Pack your bags, let's hit the trail,
With fruit hats on, we cannot fail.
Mangoes dance, so do our feet,
Chasing adventure, what a treat!

In the jungle, coconuts fall,
We laugh and dodge them, oh what a ball!
Riding bananas, we swing and sway,
Laughter echoing, come what may!

Silly monkeys play peek-a-boo,
While berries giggle, saying "Join our crew!"
Swinging from vines, we shout hurray,
In our lush world, we want to stay!

Let's gather stories, wild and free,
Where every moment's pure jubilee.
With juicy smiles and hearts so light,
Lush adventures await us, day and night!

Tasting the World Anew

Globetrotters unite, forks in the air,
Every bite's a dance, and we don't care!
Sushi spins, pasta twirls with grace,
Curry's warm hug is our favorite place.

Chocolates whisper secrets so sweet,
While tacos play maracas, can't be beat.
Pizza slices salute with a crusty cheer,
Flavor explosions, bring it here, bring it near!

From markets buzzing to trucks on the run,
Sampling flavors, oh what fun!
Cakes that giggle and pies that sing,
In this tasting game, we're all the king!

So let's feast boldly, explore with delight,
Each morsel a treasure, from day until night.
With forks raised high, let's conquer this view,
In this great big world, we taste it anew!

Threads of Sweetness

In the land of sugar plums,
Where laughter hums and drums,
I tried to bake a pie today,
But ended up with a souffle of clay.

The berries danced, the chocolate swirled,
A mess of joy, my apron twirled,
I grew a beard of whipped cream fluff,
And everyone said, 'That's more than enough!'

I served my guests a fruity glitch,
With gummy bears that did a hitch,
They laughed so hard they spilled their tea,
As my kitchen turned to jubilee!

So here's to spills, and silly fun,
In this sweet realm, we're never done,
A sprinkle here, a giggle there,
Life's a treat, beyond compare!

Honeyed Reflections

When life gives you a tin of bees,
Don't fret, just dance and shake your knees,
I tried to catch their honeyed flight,
But ended up in quite the fright!

With honey dripping from my chin,
I made a mess, oh where to begin?
The neighbors peered and shook their heads,
As sticky dreams turned into spreads.

My toast became a syrup lake,
And all my thoughts began to shake,
Do ants have parties, I wonder how?
Maybe they're coming for my chow!

So raise a toast to sweet blunders,
Life's syrupy moments with loud thunders,
Embrace the stick, the laughter wide,
In this honeyed life, let joy collide!

Orchard Allure

In an orchard where the apples grin,
I swung a basket, let the picking begin,
But alas, a rogue pear rolled away,
Turning my hunt into a fruit ballet!

The trees laughed loudly as I tripped,
With every step, my basket flipped,
I called for help, but who would come?
Just a squirrel with nuts, and a bit of gum!

I climbed a branch, oh what a scene,
Caught in the branches, stuck like a bean,
The fruits around chuckled and twirled,
As I hung there, my dreams unfurled.

So here's to orchards and fallen fruit,
To tangled limbs, and stubborn loot,
Life's a picnic, with apples so sweet,
Just watch your step, and enjoy the treat!

Richness in Simplicity

In a world where muffins reign supreme,
I had an idea, or so it would seem,
I mixed and mashed, went with the flow,
Until I found a cupcake in my shoe!

With flour on my nose and batter in hair,
I hosted a feast, but oh, was it rare,
The donuts rolled in, claiming the floor,
While my cookies collaborated and started a war!

The sprinkles spilled like confetti's fate,
As I laughed with joy at my kitchen's state,
Simplicity wrapped in a colorful bite,
Who knew joy could come from such a sight?

So here's to kitchens, to laughter and fun,
To simple delights and friendships begun,
In this sweet chaos, I'll find my way,
To savor each silly and glorious day!

Vivid Ripeness

In the orchard, fruit does dance,
Cherries giggle, given a chance.
Lemons wink from the sunny hill,
Bananas slip, oh what a thrill!

Peaches whisper in the breeze,
Melons tease with juicy ease.
Berries boast a vibrant hue,
All fruits gather, what a view!

In this setting, laughter sprawls,
Orange jests echo through the halls.
Grapes unite, play hide and seek,
While kumquats sing, oh so chic!

Each bite's a joke, a tasty spree,
Nature's jesters, wild and free.
Laughing fruits in every lane,
Making life a sweet champagne!

Tangy Tales

Lemons rolling down the street,
Telling tales with zesty beat.
Grapefruits giggle, spinning round,
In a citrus fair, joy is found.

Limes share secrets, oh so sly,
While oranges play, oh me, oh my!
Kiwis climb trees just for fun,
Life's a ride, we've just begun!

Pineapples crown, feeling grand,
Tropical dreams, let's make a band!
Fruit puns echo, laughter flows,
Dance to the rhythm, everybody knows!

With each slice, a story grows,
Whimsical nights beneath the bows.
Sip the juice, embrace the cheer,
In every drop, the fun is near!

Pearlescent Sunrises

Morning breaks with fruits aglow,
Berry blushes put on a show.
Banana rays, golden and bright,
Sun-kissed moments, sheer delight.

Pineapples hail the glowing dawn,
Melon dreams on the green lawn.
Peaches glow like morning light,
With every bite, the world feels right!

Strawberries wear their ruby best,
In the orchards, they laugh and jest.
Oranges spread their cheerful beams,
Each slice unlocks tasty dreams.

Through painted skies, colors collide,
Juicy wonders, nothing to hide.
In this garden of delight,
Life's a party, day and night!

Euphoria in Every Drop

Sipping nectar, laughter flows,
Tropic breezes, love bestows.
Sugar rush from peaches bright,
Zesty giggles, pure delight.

Juicy squirt in the summer sun,
Splash of flavor, oh what fun!
Mango melodies in the air,
Every drink, a fruity flair!

Coconut whispers, soft and smooth,
Banana shakes that simply groove.
Every drop, a chuckle shared,
Liquid laughter, no one scared!

In this garden, smiles do blend,
Nature's bounty, round the bend.
So raise your glass, let's make a toast,
To sweetened life, we love the most!

Juxtaposition of Juices

In a blender, fruits collide,
Orange laughs, as grapes abide.
Bananas slip, and lemons scream,
Together they blend in a smoothie dream.

Melon wonders if it's a fruit,
While veggies boast their leafy suit.
Cucumbers quip, 'We're in disguise!'
In the juicer, it's chaos—oh, what a surprise!

Strawberries dance, on the rim so fine,
Raspberry swirls say, 'This drink is divine!'
Kiwis giggle, 'We're tart yet sweet!'
Come sip this potion, oh what a treat!

Peach bemoans, 'I'm too fuzzy,' it seems,
While lemons just beam, fulfilling our dreams.
In this wacky mix, the taste buds rejoice,
What a flavorful party—let's raise our voice!

Pomegranate Promises

Pomegranates wear crowns, bursting with seeds,
Each one a promise, fulfilling our needs.
With a crack and a splash, juice drips like gold,
These ruby-red treasures are daring and bold.

The seeds jump like popcorn, they scatter around,
Why are they so eager to leap from the ground?
They whisper, 'We're juicy, delightful, and fun!'
Come grab your spoon, let's eat everyone!

A salad of giggles, an explosion of zest,
Plop some in yogurt, you'll surely be blessed.
Forget about calories; let happiness reign,
With every sweet seed, say goodbye to your pain!

So here's to the party of crimson delight,
With pomegranate joy, we'll dance through the night!
Let sweetness unite us, in laughter and cheer,
Join hands with these fruits; the fun's drawing near!

Squeezed Moments

Squeeze the day from a lemon's eye,
Watch the juice trickle; oh my, oh my!
An orange rolls over, 'What's this fuss?'
'Chill out, brother; it's all about us!'

A citrus debate, so juicy, so bright,
Lime jumps in, 'Let's party tonight!'
With a dash of salt and a splash of cheer,
We'll make the best drinks, just lend me your ear.

Tomato frowns, 'I'm not in the mix,'
'Oh yes, you can be, just give it a flick!'
Blend up some salsa as easy as pie,
Everyone loves a good dip; don't ask me why!

So squeeze out the moments; don't let them hide,
Invite all the flavors, let laughter abide.
The blender's your friend, so let's make a toast,
To the juicy adventures we love the most!

Bounty of Being

In the orchard, fruits scamper, so free,
With apple advice and peach philosophy.
'You are what you eat,' the bananas all shout,
'And we're going to peel it all right out!'

The grapes gossip sweetly, 'Have you heard the news?'
A cherry laughs, 'These folks really amuse!'
An avocado's lounging, all mellow and green,
While broccoli beams, feeling fit and keen.

Let's throw a bash with this harvest so bright,
Fruit punch and laughter make everything right.
With berries and nuts all mingling around,
A bounty of joy can so easily be found!

So raise up your glasses filled high to the brim,
Life's fruity concoctions—let's dive right in!
In the garden of flavors, we dance without cares,
Savoring life as the fun always wears!

Tangy Whispers of Joy

Lemons laugh, they twist and twirl,
A citrus dance that makes me whirl.
Limes join in, they have a shout,
Together, joy is what it's about.

Grapes tell tales of raucous days,
In wine-stained laughter, life's a blaze.
Peaches peel with cheeky grins,
In the fruit bowl, everyone wins!

Oranges giggle, their zest so bright,
Sunshine in slices, pure delight.
Cherries chuckle, sweet and round,
In the humor of fruit, joy is found!

Kiwi whispers, fuzzy and bold,
Tales of adventures yet untold.
Mix and mingle, create a cheer,
In a bowl of fruit; the fun is here!

Juicy Adventures

Strawberries sprint in the morning sun,
Racing to breakfast, oh what fun!
Watermelon splashes, a summer delight,
Juicy humor, a tasty bite.

Pineapple yells, 'I'm the king of sweet!'
With a crown of leaves, he can't be beat.
Bananas slip, they tumble around,
In this wacky circus, joy abounds!

Raspberries giggle, they're bursting with cheer,
A berry brigade, they all draw near.
Fruit salad shenanigans are hard to tame,
In every spoonful, laughter's the game!

Coconuts chuckle, shaking their heads,
"Life's just a coconut, no need for beds!"
Mix up a smoothie, blend it with zest,
In this juicy escapade, we're all blessed!

The Essence of Living

Life's like a cupcake, frosted with glee,
Sprinkles of laughter, come dance with me!
Bite into joy, let the flavors burst,
In this sweet chaos, we're all well-versed.

Chocolate chips tumble, they can't stay still,
Cookies unite for a baking thrill.
Frosting's a clown, giggling with glee,
In this kitchen circus, we're wild and free!

Brownies bounce, oh, what a sight,
In laughter and sweetness, we take flight.
Pies spin tales of dreams and fun,
In every slice, the laughter's never done!

So grab a fork, let's join the feast,
With dessert delights, we're never least.
In the essence of living, we find our way,
With sugar and spice, we celebrate each day!

Pulp of Experience

In the blender of life, we whirl around,
Fruitful adventures, laughter's the sound.
Strawberry smoothies, with a twist of lime,
In every slurp, we're friends in time.

Peeling a banana, what do I find?
A silly sticker that's oh-so-kind!
Mangoes whisper secrets of the sun,
In juicy tales, we all become one.

Apples bobbing in a playful race,
Each splash a giggle, a fruity embrace.
Fruits in a frenzy, let's toss 'em high,
In the pulp of experience, we reach the sky!

So squeeze out the fun, don't let it fade,
With every sweet moment, memories are made.
In this juicy journey, let's take a bite,
For life is a banquet, filled with delight!

Sun-kissed Whispers of Delight

In a world where fruit stains shirts,
Giggles burst like lemon tarts.
Grapes wear shoes of fluffy dough,
Dancing fast on lemon glow.

Silly squirrels chase after pies,
Bananas wear ridiculous ties.
Mangoes smile with cheeky grace,
As oranges roll in a race.

Jellybeans parade in the sun,
Pineapple hats, oh what fun!
Strawberries toss confetti bright,
Guava skips in morning light.

Coconut winks from afar,
Inviting all to grab a jar.
With laughter bursting, it's a spree,
Join the feast and dance with glee!

The Tang of Tomorrow

Next week's brunch is a bright affair,
With jelly spread beyond compare.
Pickles shimmy on the bread,
While cupcakes munch the crumbs instead.

Radishes plot a playful charm,
Carrots strut with extra harm.
Berries giggle, twirl, and flip,
Crafting dreams for a tasty trip.

Yet lettuce whispers, 'hold the phone,'
As dressing claims the perfect throne.
While lemons scatter seeds of cheer,
Popcorn kernels scream, 'We're here!'

Tomorrow waits with zestful cheer,
It's a circus with snacks, oh dear!
Embrace the whimsy, don't delay,
Taste the fun, come what may!

A Symphony of Sweetness

In a kitchen, pots collide,
Sugar cackles, flour slides.
Chocolate sings a joyful tune,
While peanut butter struts by noon.

Cakes are swirling in a spin,
With sprinkles laughing, bright akin.
Marshmallows float like silly dreams,
In a bowl of fantastical themes.

Whipped cream's jazzing, thick and light,
With cherries swirling, oh what a sight!
Cookies tap their toes in time,
Frosting rhymes alongside the chime.

Pudding softens, smooth and sweet,
Even veggies tap their feet.
In this symphony, oh so grand,
Give in to joy, take a stand!

Vibrancy in the Mundane

A dull carrot dreams of a ball,
While pasta prances, short and tall.
Broccoli wears its frilly crown,
While radishes sit, laughing down.

On the counter, a pickle spins,
Salsa grins as the fun begins.
Coffee beans participate with flair,
Making ordinary moments rare.

The toast pops up, a golden knight,
Butter glimmers, oh what a sight!
Jam chuckles in a fruity jig,
As toast dons its berry wig.

Even veggies in a bowl,
Join the party, play a role.
In the mundane, find the delight,
As every bite feels just right!

www.ingramcontent.com/pod-product-compliance
Lightning Source LLC
Chambersburg PA
CBHW050306120526
44590CB00016B/2512